Lunar Rover Vehicle Traverses:
An artist's concept of the Apollo 15 landing site shows the travel plan for the lunar car Rover.

To all my grandchildren
and to all the children of the blue planet

Anniversary Expanded Edition—First Printing

"Where there is no vision, the people perish."

The Vision Forum, Inc.
4719 Blanco Rd., San Antonio, Texas 78212
1-800-440-0022
www.visionforum.com

Distributed by The Vision Forum, Inc. and

Master Books
A Division of New Leaf Press
P.O. Box 726
Green Forest, Arkansas 72638

ISBN 1-929241-98-4

Printed in the United States of America

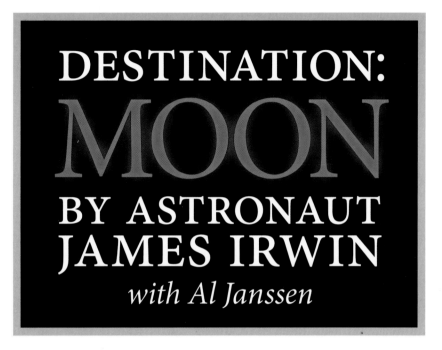

DESTINATION: MOON

BY ASTRONAUT JAMES IRWIN

with Al Janssen

*Fifteenth Anniversary
Expanded Edition*

THE VISION FORUM, INC.
SAN ANTONIO, TEXAS

TESTIMONY TO COL. JAMES IRWIN AND 'DESTINATION: MOON'

Throughout the course of his life, astronaut Jim Irwin touched the lives of diverse people from around the world. His firm faith in Jesus Christ, his bold experiences as an explorer—both on Earth and in outer space—and his love for his fellow man opened up many doors to share his life message with others. Below are just a few of the remarkable testimonies of gratitude to Colonel Irwin, from friends and admirers.

Jim Irwin was a great scientist, and a great astronaut, but he was an even a greater Christian. Because of his faith in God, we can be assured he is in Heaven, and instead of viewing the Earth from the perspective of the moon, he can see the whole universe from his new eternal home!

THE REVEREND BILLY GRAHAM

In April 1966, NASA selected Jim Irwin and me as Apollo astronauts. We moved our families to Houston, Texas and started our training at the Manned Spacecraft Center. In *Destination: Moon*, Jim has sufficiently captured the hard work, intensity, diligence to detail, and perseverance it took to prepare for a trip to the moon.

I had the pleasure of officering next to Jim during our days of training and support work. It was obvious to me that Jim would be one of the first of our group of nineteen to fly to the moon. His dedication to the task and his superb knowledge of the space systems made Jim an easy choice to be on one of the coveted flights to the moon.

Destination: Moon clearly captures the thrill of a lunar adventure. Jim and Dave blazed the trail for the rest of us who followed them. They were the first to stay three days on the lunar surface, first to use the Lunar Rover, first to land in the mountains of the moon, and first to use the lunar drill.

Jim had a very moving spiritual encounter with God during his lunar stay. He truly experienced the psalmist's words, "The Heavens declare the glory of God, and the skies proclaim the works of His hands." It was my privilege to work with Jim and High Flight Foundation on numerous occasions. Jim's life, this book, and his testimony to God's grace and goodness will have a lasting influence on many people.

GEN. CHARLIE DUKE
Lunar Module Pilot, Apollo 16

Destination: Moon is the inspiring account of Jim Irwin's historic voyage to the moon and his walk on the moon's surface. Written with authority and scientific accuracy, yet also with a sense of awe and wonder, it's a story that exemplifies bravery, technology, and Jim's personal encounter with God. A great read and wonderful keepsake, I enthusiastically recommend *Destination: Moon*.

WILLIAM L. ARMSTRONG
United States Senator

When I hear any story of a great journey, I want to make the journey, too. When someone who has made the journey is telling the story, I feel like I have gone there myself. Before I was ever able to travel to the streets of Paris, France, the beaches of Hawaii, or to the rides in Disneyland, I heard stories of those places from friends who had just been there. I felt like I had made the trip through their recollections.

James Irwin took a magnificent trip to the moon. He ramped all over a place called Hadley/Appenine mountains, studied its riles and picked up its rocks. He rode in an electric car for miles, slept for three nights, and ate breakfast, lunch, and dinner on a place which can be thought of as, more or less, another planet. On almost any night, you can look up into the sky and find the spot—right *there*—where James and his friend Dave had a fabulous campout on the moon.

After reading *Destination: Moon*, you may feel like you made the trip with astronaut Irwin. I did. Maybe, you will want to make the trip for real yourself someday. I have not done that. However, you can. Someday!

TOM HANKS
Actor, "Apollo 13"

Jim Irwin's adventures on the moon made him an American hero. His use of those adventures to glorify God and point others to Christ make him a Christian hero.

DR. JOHN MORRIS
President, Institute for Creation Research

[James Irwin's] life has enriched mine through his loving, caring, gracious, sensitive spirit. I have been especially impressed with his vision to take the Gospel to the world through the flags which he took with him to the moon.

BILL BRIGHT
Campus Crusade for Christ

In 1968, as Apollo 8 circled the moon, the astronauts read Genesis 1 for the whole world to hear. What a "spine chilling" experience if you have the opportunity to hear those word as they were read from space. At that time, Jim Irwin, one of the few selected by NASA to be an astronaut in the Apollo program, did not know that he would be chosen to actually walk on the Moon in 1971. I can't imagine what it must have been like to praise the God of creation while standing on the moon. However, Jim Irwin has left a legacy in this book to enable each one of us to have a sense of what this must have been like. Experience the thrill of landing on the moon—but most of all, experience the joy of praising the Creator while standing on the moon with Jim Irwin. This is an exciting journey for children and adults alike.

KEN HAM
President, Answers in Genesis

Jim Irwin's relationship to the Summit was always close. I view him not only as superb astronaut but a true "Lab Scientist." He went to the moon to check out the various theories regarding the amount of dust on the moon and actually found it to be 3" instead of the fourteen to twenty-seven feet, as announced by certain philosophers of science. This is science in its truest form—and, as it turns out, not contrary to Genesis, either.

DR. DAVID A. NOEBEL
President, Summit Ministries

A quarter of a million miles away while standing in the lunar dust, Jim Irwin looked back at the Earth and saw a blue, white, brown, and green living, breathing orb suspended in the black vacuum of space. He knew in his soul that there was a divine hand that created it all. Jim Irwin fulfilled a dream that day by journeying as high as the stars and he would never be the same, how could anyone. Knowing Jim as a friend has inspired me in my life's journey to reach higher than I ever would. Come join Jim on this incredible adventure and slip the surly bonds of Earth and touch the face of God.

BOB CORNUKE
President, BASE Institute

It was a great privilege to know James Irwin and to travel overseas with him. His life-commitment to Jesus Christ was a powerful motivation in sharing his experience as an astronaut. I know that many lives were deeply touched wherever he went. While his trip to the moon was a grand feat in his life, his ultimate destination in eternity with God and with his Savior is what shaped his commitment.

DR. RAVI K. ZACHARIAS
President, Ravi Zacharias International Ministries

We were deeply saddened by the news of the passing away of Colonel James Irwin [on August 8, 1991]. His illustrious achievement as an astronaut and his deep faith and devotion, to the service of God, made him an inspiring figure who will be mourned by all people in all parts of the world. As we share with you your moment of sadness, we send to you our heartfelt condolences and we pray to God to grant you solace and forbearance.

KING HUSSEIN I OF JORDAN

Colonel James Benson Irwin
March 17, 1930 - August 8, 1991

"Precious in the sight of the LORD is the death of his saints."
Psalm 116:15

FOREWORD

"The lesser light to rule over the night." Genesis 1:16

In 1971, my father was working for the President of the United States. One day, he was invited to take our whole family to Cape Canaveral to meet with NASA officials and participate in a guided tour of the facilities. This included a special peek into the Apollo 15 capsule, which was then scheduled to carry three very brave men on the next manned mission to the moon.

The visit was electrifying. My boyish imagination was fired, and a lifetime of passion for science and discovery was inaugurated. At once I knew that somehow my mission in life would include the exploration and study of creation. I can still feel that boyish enthusiasm, that sense of hope and adventure when I look back on the day my father introduced me to the Apollo 15 mission and the concept of space travel. Over thirty years later, I now have the honor to introduce you to one of the men whose space mission so profoundly influenced me as a boy.

Col. Jim Irwin was not merely the Lunar Module pilot for Apollo 15, he was the eighth man in the history of the universe to set foot on the moon. What a remarkable accomplishment! What a gift! But the eighth man ever to walk on the moon viewed his personal accomplishment as insignificant compared to the infinitely glorious accomplishments of the extraordinary Creator whom he served and who, by the very power of His Word, created the moon itself.

In fact, the eighth man to walk on the moon took the entire Bible seriously because he took its Author seriously. He rejoiced in the Genesis account of origins. He believed that God had created the world in six twenty-four-hour days. He accepted as scientific and historical fact that the moon itself was created on Day Four, and was thus not the result of a Big Bang or the product of millions of years of cosmic evolution. Through his actions and his firm conviction in the accuracy of God's Word, Col. Irwin left for future generations a thrilling legacy that there is no conflict between science and faith, no tension between the origins of the moon and the Genesis account of creation.

After his return to Earth, Astronaut Jim Irwin would spend the rest of his life on another amazing journey designed to give glory to Jesus Christ, the Creator of the moon. As the founder of the High Flight Foundation, Jim embarked on a journey of evangelism and discovery that not only brought him to the remote corners of the Earth, but to the very Mountains of Ararat in search of Noah's Ark.

Adventurer, evangelist, scientist, test pilot, father—Apollo Astronaut Jim Irwin was all of these things, and more. As we approach the twenty-fifth anniversary of the historic, half-million mile journey which brought him to the very surface of the moon, it is important to stop and remember the most remarkable message of Jim Irwin's life. This message is best summarized by the maxim, which he, as the eighth man on the moon, shared with tens of thousands of children around the globe. It was this:

"Jesus walking on Earth is more important than man walking on the moon."

In 1971, I was one of those little boys who began to look at the stars and dream big dreams because of the work of Col. Jim Irwin and the astronauts of his day. Like other little boys, I admired the men of the Apollo program and imagined that I, too, would someday be an astronaut or astronomer on the cusp of some great new discovery. I look back on that time with the deepest of gratitude, realizing that God used the historic journeys of those men to put a hunger in my soul, not merely for creation, but for the God of creation. This hunger ultimately resulted for me in the greatest discovery a man can make: a personal knowledge of the Creator of the moon, our only God and Savior, the Lord Jesus Christ.

It is my sincere prayer that the republication of this very special book on the fifteenth anniversary of the original will serve as an inspiration to a new generation of children who will rise up and recognize the beautiful harmony between the Christian faith and science. May they embrace as a deep abiding conviction the glorious truth that all things are possible through Jesus Christ, even the most remarkable journeys of discovery to the depths of His cosmos and the very surface of "the lesser light to rule over the night," His moon.

Doug Phillips
President, The Vision Forum, Inc.
San Antonio, Texas
September 2004

PROLOGUE

When you lean far back and look up, you can see the Earth like a beautiful, fragile Christmas tree ornament hanging against the blackness of space. It's as if you could reach out and hold it in your hand. That's a feeling, a perception, I had never anticipated. And I don't think it's blasphemous for me to say I felt I was seeing the Earth with the eyes of God.

But the actual journey which brought me to the moon, began long before my rocket blasted off from Earth. It was a roundabout and amazing journey, a journey so unexpected and remarkable that it can only be explained as the providential direction of God in my life.

Before the flight of Apollo 15, I considered myself a technician, a test pilot, the operator of a spacecraft—really a nuts-and-bolts type. And I didn't have an unblemished record, either. I had made mistakes, goofed up many times, had my ups and downs, physically and spiritually. But on my third try, just as I reached the age limit, I was accepted into the astronaut program. This was the most elite group in the service. What a great honor. But even then, I had no idea that I would ever be chosen to actually go to the moon.

When I was selected as an astronaut, it was something of a miracle that I was still in the Air Force. I had squeaked into Annapolis with a fraction of a point to spare on the substantiating examination. Then, before I had even graduated from the Naval Academy, I was ready to give that up. The Navy was so outmoded, so old-fashioned in its policies that I didn't want any part of that branch of the service. It seemed ridiculous to spend so much time at sea, for example. Sure, it was nice to go for a short boat ride, but why spend six months or a year away from your family? There were so many more interesting things to do on land—or even in the air.

It was providential that the Air Force was created in 1949, and that they were looking for young officers. The Air Force was able to take twenty percent of our class at Annapolis. Fortunately, I drew a low number. If I had stuck in the Navy, I probably would have served the minimum time and then resigned.

As it turned out, I had some fantastic opportunities in the Air Force. I was even assigned to be the first and only test pilot on the world's highest- and fastest-flying airplane, the YF-12A, which made me so proud that I thought I was the hottest test pilot in the sky. But truthfully, throughout most of my Air Force career, I was sorry I hadn't gotten out of the service back in 1955 and gone with a commercial airline. At the time I thought that life would be more satisfying if I could be a simple airline pilot until the age of sixty-five and then just retire. I couldn't think of a more relaxing life, particularly for a man like me who loves to fly. I would make enough money and still have a lot of free time.

I can't imagine life without flying now, but it wasn't an instant love affair. During my pilot training in Hondo, Texas, I came to the conclusion that I didn't care much for it. I had had about ten hours when I decided I wasn't cut out to be a pilot. Aviation wasn't challenging or exciting. I was uncomfortable in the bumpy Texas air. It didn't make me airsick, but I didn't feel comfortable.

I also didn't think I had any outstanding aptitude for flying. I was probably average. But I was relaxed and I slept a whole lot. Half the guys in my little flight group washed out. I've always thought that the only reason I didn't wash out was because I didn't clutch up. Maybe the fact that I wasn't particularly interested in flying made it easier to go through with it. Another important factor in my success was a great guy from south Texas named Ed Siers who was my flight instructor. Ed probably had fifteen or twenty hours at the time; he was an old crop-duster and had done all types of flying. "We'll try to work this thing out," he said. "I'll try to find some smooth air for you."

Ed didn't find much smooth air, but he took me through my training period. When I was knocked out with pneumonia and had lost two weeks, he even volunteered to fly with me on weekends to help me catch up. So I stuck with it and graduated with my class.

As much as I like Ed, I discovered something new about myself when I soloed. It was a great relief to get into an airplane by myself, with no instructor along. It was good to be rid of all that noise in the back seat. I flew better when I could get up there in the sky, close to God, all by myself. That solitude was and is complete joy for me.

After I had gotten my wings, I picked an assignment at the Air Force base in Yuma, Arizona. When I got to Yuma, I saw P-51s there on the runway. Just seeing them was all it took. Flying that 51 really caught me by surprise. It opened up a whole new thrill for me in flying. Suddenly I came into my own. All the tedium and boredom and everything else I had been trying to escape was behind me. I was hooked.

But in those years, my career was forever being blocked. I was grounded many times for violations—a little too relaxed and high-spirited maybe. And then I almost wiped out in a terrible air accident. I thought I'd lost my chance to fly the YF-12A, the test pilot's dream. When I had recovered sufficiently to report for duty, they told me, "No, Captain Irwin. You have had a concussion. You have even had amnesia. We can't let you fly for at least a year while we completely evaluate you."

In 1963, I applied to NASA's space program, but they turned me down. I believe they felt my accident was too recent. The second time around, NASA was looking for scientists with doctorates and I couldn't qualify. I was hounded by the history of my injury and fast approaching the age limit for astronauts. In 1966, I made one last desperate effort.

My boss at the Air Defense Command in Colorado Springs, Col. Wilton Earle, went to bat for me. He must have contacted all the generals he had ever known in the Air Force. I don't know what he told them, but obviously it had a powerful effect. It was fortunate for me that this time around, in the selection of the fifth group, they picked nineteen, the largest number ever. There were examinations and interviews and physicals and all the rest of it, and finally the announcements were made. Jim Irwin was selected.

This was the highest honor I could imagine. I had only one way of explaining this mind-boggling thing that had happened to me. But the explanation did not fully come to me until the flight of Apollo 15 was over and I had a chance to fully reflect on what God had done in my life. The Lord wanted me to go to the moon so I could come back and do something more important with my life than fly airplanes. During the years of training and the many months of competition with the other astronauts for the assignment as a primary crewman, I had been so absorbed in preparing for the scientific flight that it never occurred to me how high the spiritual flight could be.

As we reached out in a physical way to the heavens, I was moved spiritually. Flying into space, I had a new sense of who I was as a man created in the image of God, of the wonder of the remarkable Earth that God created for man to inhabit, and of the very presence of my Creator.

As I headed into the cosmos, I became increasingly aware of how different my present circumstances were from the reality of life on Earth. Within my very spirit, I sensed the beginning of a glorious change taking place inside of me. Looking back at that spaceship we call Earth, I was touched by a desire to convince man that he is a unique creature made in the image of God, and that he must learn to honor God and love his fellow man.

During this sort of flight, you are too busy to fully reflect on the splendor of space or even to appreciate the deep spiritual significance and honor of man journeying into the heavens. But the ultimate effect this journey had on me was to reshape my very faith in God. Throughout my space journey, I felt an overwhelming sense of the presence of God, especially on the moon itself. I felt His spirit more closely than I have ever felt it on Earth. Standing on the moon, with the expanse of space before me, I rejoiced in the nearness of God. And when our astronaut team was struggling with the difficult tasks, I prayed and the Lord always sent an immediate answer.

I am not the only astronaut to be affected by this experience on the moon and in space. Every man who goes to the moon is deeply affected, one way or another, by the journey. The effect on me was to draw me closer to my God, Jesus Christ.

I think there are things that God does not intend man to understand, things that man is to take on faith. Believing in the Creator and taking Him at His word is a matter of faith. But the Bible teaches that the very heavens declare the glory of God, even His eternal power and godhead, such that man is without excuse. Man was designed to respond to his Creator, and the Bible teaches that Jesus Christ, the second person of the Trinity, was the very Creator of the universe. That is why nothing will ever surpass the beauty and simplicity of the message of the Gospel. I hate to see people confused about it.

It took me about a month to discover what had happened inside me. When I first talked to people about Apollo 15, I would tell them anything they wanted to know about space, about the scientific side. The scientific voyage of discovery was, after all, what NASA had invested years preparing us to accomplish. Shortly after the flight, we started our visits around the world—goodwill missions directed by the President. Al, Dave, and I participated as a crew on these occasions. They were designed to be scientific exchanges. I didn't have the satisfaction of telling the complete story and sharing my own religious experience.

However, when we visited Italy, there were many questions at the press conference about the religious implications of the trip to the moon. Since Dave and Al considered me the preacher, I answered the questions. In the weeks, months, and years that followed, I had the great satisfaction of being able to share the complete message. I started working unofficially on weekends, trying not to create a problem for NASA. I received so much encouragement from the churches where I had been speaking, and from Mary and the children to go ahead with this work, that there has been a growing conviction about my commitment and a strengthening of my message. I feel a terrific compulsion to hit as hard as I can while I can be useful, before my fame fades.

The response from people everywhere has been tremendously moving. Everybody wants to talk to a man who has been to the moon. They think that since he has seen something they have not seen and will never see, he must know something they do not know. They are interested in the scientific voyage, but they are also interested in the spiritual voyage. They are interested in what happened inside us, in our hearts and souls. They can't go to the moon, but they can take this flight.

When I came back from the flight, I was baptized at the Nassau Bay Baptist Church in Houston with my daughter Jill. I had accepted Christ when I was a boy of eleven in New Port Richey, Florida, at a revival meeting, but I didn't stay as close to the Lord as I should have. But after the flight, the power of God was working in me and I was possessed by a growing feeling that God did have a new mission for me.

I tell people that God has a plan for them. I say that if God controls the universe with such infinite precision, controlling all the motion of the planets and the stars, this is the working out of a perfect plan for outer space. I believe that He has the perfect plan for the inner space of man, the spirit of man. This plan was manifest when He sent His son Jesus Christ to die for us, to forgive our sins, and to show us He has a plan for our lives.

It seems plain to me that the hand of God has been in my life as far back as I am able to remember. I think Providence has been a factor in every important thing that has ever happened to me. As strange as it sounds, my flight on Apollo 15 was the fulfillment of a dream I had all my life. I have talked of wanting to go to the moon since I was a young boy. My mother says that she remembers this, and some old neighbors of ours whom she talked to recently also remembered that when I was a little boy I used to point up to the moon and say, "I'm going to go up there someday."

I probably said this, but I don't know how much confidence I had that I would be able to do it. Reverses along the way made it seem unlikely that I was headed in this direction. When it happened, I felt that I was doing something I had always wanted to do. But the most startling thing to me now is not that I have made the flight but what the flight has done to me. God has changed my life.

On the mountains of the moon, I had an opportunity to quote a favorite Psalm: "I will lift up mine eyes unto the hills, from whence cometh my help." As I quoted, I had the impulse to add, "But of course, we get quite a bit from Houston, too." This incredible flight that we made with help from Houston is one of the extraordinary technological achievements in the history of man. I can believe it only because I understand it and can retrace it step by step. As I tell this story of the scientific voyage of Apollo 15, I will also try to tell the story of that other voyage I made with the help of God.

ASTRONAUT JAMES IRWIN

DESTINATION:
MOON

2

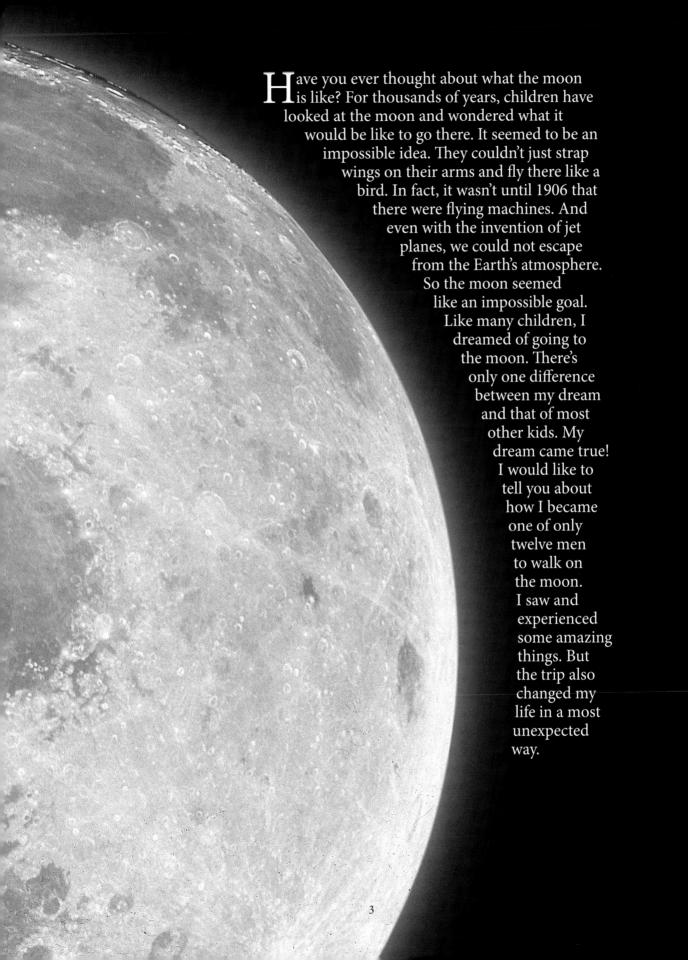

Have you ever thought about what the moon is like? For thousands of years, children have looked at the moon and wondered what it would be like to go there. It seemed to be an impossible idea. They couldn't just strap wings on their arms and fly there like a bird. In fact, it wasn't until 1906 that there were flying machines. And even with the invention of jet planes, we could not escape from the Earth's atmosphere. So the moon seemed like an impossible goal. Like many children, I dreamed of going to the moon. There's only one difference between my dream and that of most other kids. My dream came true! I would like to tell you about how I became one of only twelve men to walk on the moon. I saw and experienced some amazing things. But the trip also changed my life in a most unexpected way.

Until 1957, space travel was only a fantasy. We could read stories about what it might be like. But that was only our imagination. Then the Soviet Union launched a satellite called Sputnik that circled the Earth many times every day. Four years later, Yuri Gagarin became the first human being to fly in space.

The first American to orbit the Earth was John Glenn. He was part of a program called Project Mercury. That was the first step toward the dream of President John F. Kennedy who challenged the United States to *commit itself to achieving the goal, before this decade is out, of landing a man on the moon and returning him safely to the Earth.*

Each trip into space was a little longer and more complicated. After Project Mercury came Gemini where two men flew together. During some of these flights, an astronaut actually left his spacecraft and floated in space.

More astronauts were added to the space program as the time for moon flights drew closer. My, how I wanted to be one of those astronauts. But there was a problem. I was teaching a student how to fly and lost control of the plane and we crashed into the desert. I was a mess—two broken legs, a broken jaw, and a banged-up head. It was so bad that the doctors wondered if I'd ever walk again. Fortunately, the student pilot also survived, though he had serious head injuries.

God was good to me and I did fly again. However, twice I applied for the space program and was turned down. They didn't tell me why, but it probably was because of my injuries from the plane crash. I was almost thirty-six-years old, the point when I would be too old to be considered as an astronaut.

Cosmonaut Yuri Gagarin was the first human to fly into space (*facing page, shown immediately prior to his historic flight on Vostok 1*). Americans Alan Shepard (*bottom left*) and Virgil Grissom (*launch, facing page*) had brief trips into space that lasted only a few minutes. Then on February 20, 1962, John Glenn (*top and middle*) orbited Earth three times on a mission that gave America's space program much-needed momentum. For the next few years, NASA had an impressive stretch of successes, including Ed White's space walk in 1965 (*below*).

There are so many things you have to learn if you want to be an astronaut. Sitting in school is not always fun. When I was bored, it helped to remember that I needed to learn these lessons if I wanted a chance to go into space.

Besides going to college, I had to learn how to fly airplanes. Then I went to a special school for test pilots, and another school for future astronauts. I learned about computers and how various rockets work. There were math and science classes. One course was called Orbital Mechanics. We learned how rockets launch satellites into space so they will stay there, orbiting the Earth.

Before I became an astronaut, I worked on a top-secret airplane called the YF-12A. This plane set speed and altitude records for the United States. But for several years, I couldn't tell anyone about this exciting work, not even my family. I'm very proud of what I did on this plane and how my work helped my country.

However, my big dream was the moon. Because of my experience, I was allowed to apply a third time for the space program. I had to take a lot of special tests, including a very complete physical examination. I guess they wanted to make sure my head wasn't too scrambled from the plane crash. It must have been all right because this time I was accepted! And just in time; another few months and I would have reached the age limit.

Jim Irwin (*fifth from left, back row*) was one of nineteen astronauts selected by NASA in April 1966. Prior to this, Jim worked on the top secret YF-12A plane (*below*).

Centrifuge training allowed astronauts to experience the physical sensations of launch and reentry. After each ride in the centrifuge, they were tested to see how their bodies responded to those pressures. Basic training classes included jungle survival school (*middle right*) and geological field trips to places like Iceland (*lower right*).

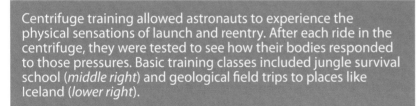

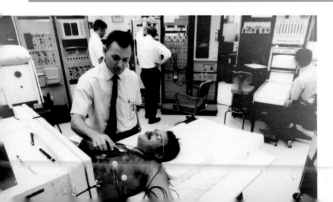

I thought I'd learned a lot before I was an astronaut. But there were five more years of training ahead before my trip into space. Sometimes I thought my brain was going to explode because of all the information I had to remember. There were classes in subjects like astronomy (study of the stars), geology (study of rocks), and spacecraft design.

Fortunately, not all of our time was spent in a classroom. We took field trips to factories that made the rockets and spacecraft. We traveled around the world in order to understand the geology of the Earth compared to what we would see on the moon. We visited planetariums and observatories to practice our identification of stars.

Athletic training was important, too. We had to stay in top shape for the physical demands of space flight. We also spent time in a centrifuge. A centrifuge is a machine that spins astronauts around in a circle very fast so that we feel the pressures we will experience during launch and return to Earth. Ever had an elephant sit on you? Well, that's how it feels when the centrifuge is going full speed.

Every aspect of space travel must be practiced. New astronauts learn the "feel" of weightlessness during zero-gravity training on an Air Force KC-135 airplane (*left*). An Apollo astronaut is lifted aboard a Coast Guard helicopter during a simulated recovery operation in the Gulf of Mexico (*below*). A Gemini pilot practices for a space walk in underwater zero-gravity training (*facing page*).

Of course, once we're in space, we are weightless. If we aren't buckled to our seats, we float. It takes a while to get used to that. After all, I doubt that any of us have floated around our home or classroom, have we? That's because we are held on the Earth by gravity.

There are two ways to learn how it feels to be weightless. One is by flying in an airplane many miles above the Earth, then pushing the plane's nose down as if you were on a roller coaster starting down a steep incline. As you go over the top, you experience weightlessness for thirty to forty seconds. We'd do this hundreds of times. Sometimes all of that motion made me sick to my stomach. But usually it was fun floating around the airplane cabin.

Astronauts also learn how to scuba dive because you can experience the sensation of weightlessness under water. Also, by adding a little weight you can feel what it's like at one-sixth of Earth's gravity, which is what we would experience on the moon.

We went to another school to learn how to fly helicopters. What do helicopters have to do with space flight? The lunar module that landed on the moon is actually a hovercraft that operates much like a helicopter.

As you can see, there was so much to do and learn that we had little time to relax. Sometimes we got very tired and missed being with our families.

After our basic training was finished, we were assigned important jobs to do. My job was to test the lunar module that would land on the moon. Many changes were made on the entire Apollo system after a tragic fire killed three astronauts. We had to know if the changes would prevent another tragedy.

I took this job very seriously. You would, too, if you knew your life depended on your work. When you're on the moon, 250,000 miles away from home, no one can rescue you if something goes wrong. Since the moon doesn't have air, water, or food, we wouldn't live very long if, for some reason, we couldn't lift off. So you want to be sure that everything will work, even under the most difficult conditions.

Testing for the lunar module was done in a thermal vacuum chamber. This is a huge room where the air is pumped out to create a vacuum. Then the room is heated to more than 250 degrees Fahrenheit, which is the temperature on the surface of the moon when it's in the sunlight. You couldn't go into this room without wearing a space suit.

It took a year to run all of the tests. Only then could the contractors build the rest of the modules needed for the lunar flights. Of all the things I did as an astronaut, I think I'm proudest of this project because it was so difficult and also so important to the space program.

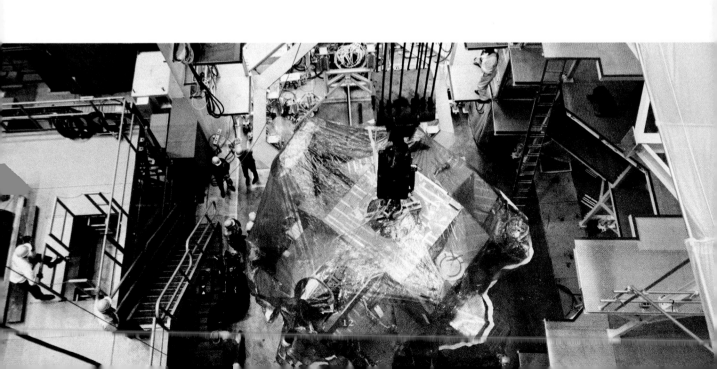

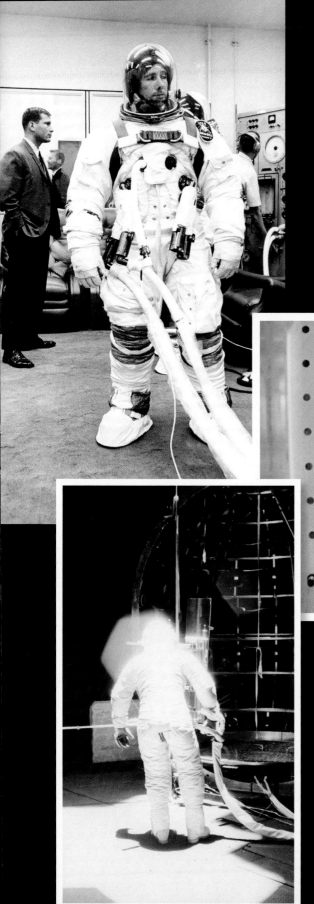

The tragic fire aboard the Apollo 1 led to extensive redesign and testing of spacecraft. A test model of the lunar module is lowered into a chamber for testing (*facing page*). Jim Irwin suited up many times for tests in the thermal vacuum chamber. The glow around a test subject (*bottom left*) is produced from carbon arc lamps designed to simulate the direct rays of the sun in space.

It was 1969, the year we had planned to land on the moon. The Apollo 10 mission was to be the final dress rehearsal. It would fly to the moon, and the lunar module would leave the command module and fly down to within fifty thousand feet of the surface.

My job was to support the crew of Apollo 10. The support team is a vital part of a mission. While the primary and backup crews train for the flight, the support team acts as their eyes to make sure all of their equipment works right.

For me, this meant visiting many factories and carefully looking over the command module, service module, and lunar module. We ran many tests to make sure everything worked. The equipment didn't leave the factory until we said it was ready.

The many parts of a rocket and spacecraft are assembled in the gigantic Vehicle Assembly Building (*facing page*). The 363-foot tall Apollo vehicle is then moved to the launch pad by a huge crawler-transporter. The primary, backup, and support teams spend a lot of time inside the command module, testing the systems and training for launch day.

Then we watched as all of the parts of the rocket and spacecraft were put together in the Vehicle Assembly Building. That's one of the world's biggest buildings and it's just three miles from the launch pad. We made sure everything was connected and worked properly. Then the rocket was moved to the launch pad. There, we checked it out again before the primary crew took over.

We apparently did our job well and the mission was a huge success. That paved the way for Apollo 11 and the historic moment two months later when Neil Armstrong became the first person to walk on the moon. I still get excited when I remember watching on television as Neil's foot touched lunar soil for the first time and he uttered the famous words, "That's one small step for man, one giant leap for mankind." I knew I had played an important role in helping to make this historic moment.

Now I wanted to take my turn to go to the moon. But I would have to wait a little longer.

I took a step closer when I was backup for Apollo 12, the second lunar landing. The backup crew trains for a mission the same way as the primary crew. If anything should happen to one of the primary crew members, the backup person is ready to step in and take over. Though I was ready, I wasn't needed for this flight.

There are many things that can go wrong in space. If we weren't so well prepared, we could easily become very afraid. The purpose of testing and training is to prevent as many mistakes and accidents as possible. But space travel is dangerous, and we all know that, even with all of the preparation, there are risks.

During Apollo 13, which was supposed to be the third landing on the moon, an oxygen tank exploded and severely damaged the service module. Oxygen, electricity, and water were lost to the command module. The three astronauts had to use the smaller lunar module as a lifeboat. Naturally, they couldn't land on the moon, and they had a very dangerous trip home.

Fortunately, a lot of people back on Earth were ready to help. Several astronauts did experiments in simulators to find out what our friends needed to do to get home safely. Then Houston Control relayed instructions to the men in space. There was a sense of teamwork as we raced the clock to try and solve some huge problems. We felt like a sports team that, through hard work, defeats an unbeaten opponent against all odds. When the Apollo 13 crew returned safely, it felt like we'd won an Olympic championship!

The explosion of
an oxygen tank on
Apollo 13's service
module made for
a very dangerous
journey home.
One problem
was a buildup
of poisonous
carbon dioxide
gas. Technicians
on the ground
designed and
tested a "mailbox"
that filtered out the
gas from the lunar
module (*below*).
Astronauts also
tested various
maneuvers in
a simulator
(*facing page*). The
damaged service
module and lunar
module were
jettisoned in space
just before Earth
reentry.

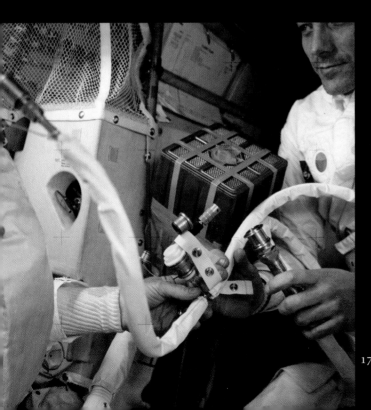

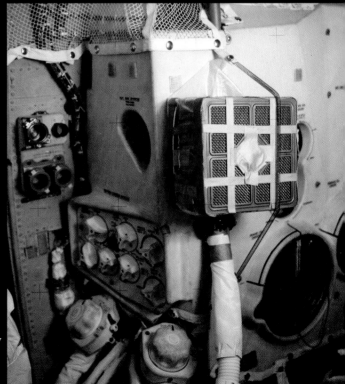

I got some great news in late 1969. I was selected to fly to the moon as part of the Apollo 15 crew. This is what I'd dreamed of for nearly forty years! Dave Scott was our mission commander, and he and I would descend to the moon. Al Worden would fly the command module and circle the moon for nearly three days while we went down for a look. We thought we'd trained hard until now. But there was a lot more to learn. For one thing, we had to take an advanced course in lunar geology. This meant more field trips to places like Alaska, Mexico, Colorado, and Hawaii (that was my favorite!). Because we were going to land in the mountains of the moon, we particularly studied volcanoes, for we thought we might find evidence of volcanic activity on the moon. Each field trip we practiced the procedures we'd use on the moon. Dave would choose a rock and set a pointer, called a gnomon, by it. Together we'd try to identify the kind of rock it was and I'd take several pictures of it. Only then did we pick up the rock and place it in a numbered bag. In this way we learned how to gather as much scientific information as possible in the short time we would have on the lunar surface.

Training for the Apollo 15 mission included (*left to right across the bottom*): collecting a core sample; water egress training; desert survival training; pulling an equipment transporter; simulating exploration at one-sixth gravity; and using a lunar drill.

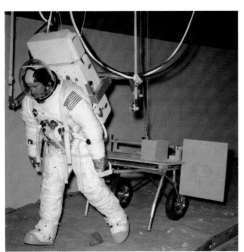

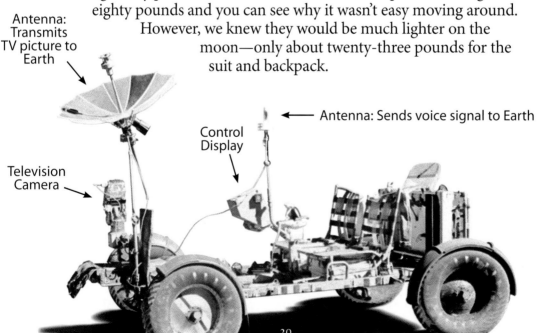

On this mission, there was a new piece of equipment to help us explore more of the moon. We would be the first astronauts to drive a car on another planet. We called it Rover and we practiced driving it a lot. That was fun, but we had to be careful. After all, it cost $8 million to build and test! We even got a special driver's license and license plate from General Motors.

Many of our practice sessions were done in the space suits. The lunar suits weigh sixty pounds on Earth. Add to that a backpack that weighs eighty pounds and you can see why it wasn't easy moving around. However, we knew they would be much lighter on the moon—only about twenty-three pounds for the suit and backpack.

Antenna:
Transmits
TV picture to
Earth

Antenna: Sends voice signal to Earth

Control
Display

Television
Camera

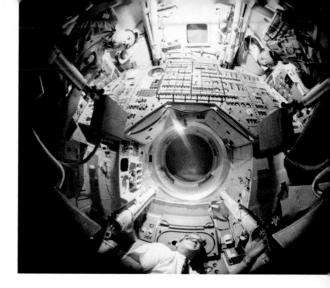

We also spent hundreds of hours in simulators. This was how we practiced flying in space. All of the things we would see could be recreated in the simulator. For instance, photos and maps of the lunar surface were used to make very realistic models. We had everything except the dust. A camera moved over the surface as we worked the controls of the lunar module, practicing landings. We saw these pictures through our windows, so it was easy to imagine what it would be like for the real trip. We also could drive Rover using the simulator.

As we continued to practice, emergencies were put in to test our skills and reactions. We'd be landing on the moon and one or more warning lights would flash. We'd have to decide whether or not to abort the landing and return to the command module. It was a little like playing a difficult video game, only much more serious. We knew that when we were on the trip for real, no one could rescue us if we got into trouble.

Simulators allowed astronauts to practice every part of their space flights. Jim Irwin and Dave Scott spent a lot of time with the Lunar Roving Vehicle, both indoors and at various outdoor locations. Training time was also spent in the command module *(top right)* and lunar module *(middle right)*.

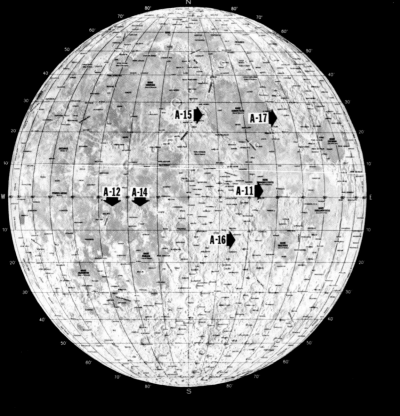

On each trip to the moon, a different landing site had been selected. Though the moon is one-fourth the size of Earth, there was so much to explore that it was decided to visit as many different kinds of places as possible.

We might compare it to an explorer coming to Earth from another planet. If that space traveler could only make five or six visits, he might go once to a mountain range, another time to a river valley, another to an ocean beach. He might make one stop in North America, another in Europe, a third in Asia. We took that same approach in our exploration of the moon.

The three landings before our flights had been in the lower, flatter areas that appear darker when we look at the moon. On our trip, it was decided to explore a mountainous area. I was thrilled with this decision because it meant we would see many new kinds of geological formations.

The choice was a site called Hadley Rille. A rille is like a canyon on Earth. This one was more than one thousand feet deep and three thousand feet across. We would explore the rille, several craters, and a thirteen-thousand-foot mountain.

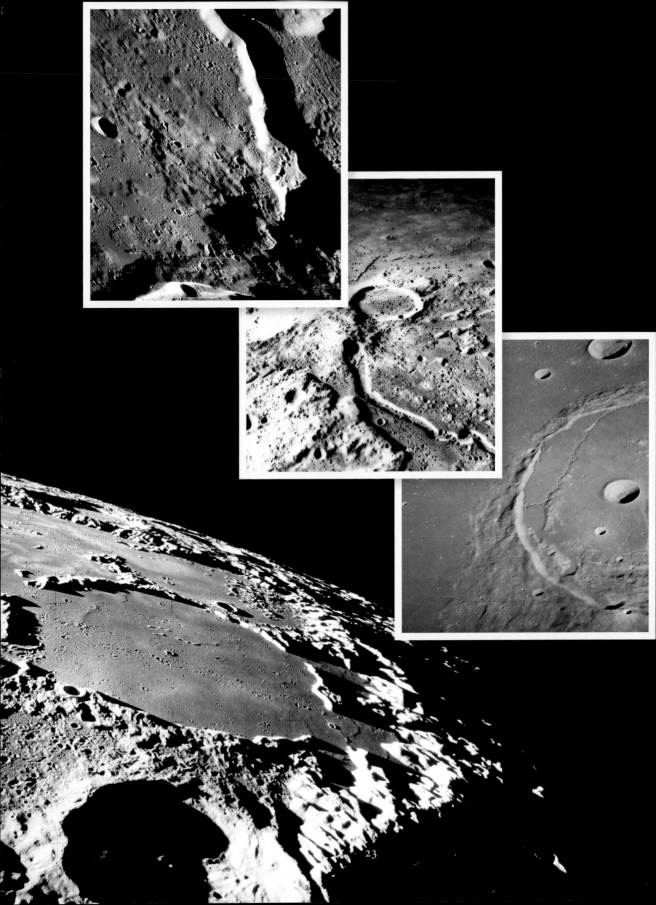

Finally, the big day arrived. It was still dark when we were awakened at 4:30 in the morning. "Okay, guys, are you ready to go to the moon?" asked Deke Slayton, our boss. You bet we were ready!

First, a doctor gave us a brief physical examination. He wanted to be sure that we were completely healthy for the trip. Fortunately, all of us checked out fine. We certainly didn't want to miss this adventure because of a cold.

Then we had breakfast—steak, scrambled eggs, and orange juice. I really enjoyed that, knowing it was the last solid meal I'd have for nearly two weeks. Surprisingly, we were all quiet. We were each thinking about what was going to happen. No one wanted to disturb another's thoughts.

After breakfast, it was time to put on our space suits. First, sensors were attached to our chests to monitor our heart rates and physical status. Then we put on long underwear and the suit. Finally, our helmets were placed over our heads and we began breathing pure oxygen.

The air we normally breathe is only about one-fifth oxygen. Nitrogen and other gases make up the rest of our air. We had to breathe pure

A big breakfast began the historic day. Then Jim suited up before breathing pure oxygen for three hours *(facing page, bottom)*. Jim had a towel draped over his helmet so he could get a little more sleep.

oxygen for three hours to get rid of the nitrogen in our bloodstream. Otherwise, it could produce dangerous bubbles in our blood, like the "bends" that scuba divers get. During this time, I tried to get a little more sleep.

Finally the call came to head for the launch pad. We had to carry a portable ventilator in one hand in order to keep breathing oxygen. Because I was the shortest, I had to hold my hose high so it didn't drag on the ground. I certainly didn't want a dirty hose!

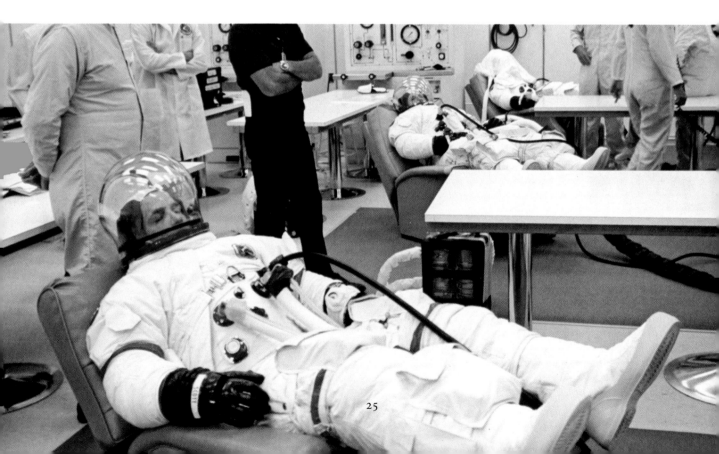

We rode an elevator up to our spacecraft, which we'd named *Endeavour*. Our seats were 360 feet off the ground. That's like going up thirty-six floors in a tall building. A crew helped us get into our couches, connect our hoses, and tighten the straps on our seat belts and shoulder harnesses. They checked electrical connections so we could talk to launch control at the Cape and to mission control in Houston.

Finally, the door was shut. It made a big clang, like the sound of a dungeon door in a movie. That's when we knew it was for real. The waiting was over; we were going to the moon!

We heard the last seconds of countdown: "Ten, nine, eight . . . three, two, one, ignition!

"You have liftoff."

THIRD STAGE
SECOND STAGE
FIRST STAGE

I still can recall all of the sensations and emotions of my trip. It's as if I am reliving it again today. When we hear "ignition" at the end of the countdown, we don't feel much. There is a muffled roar and just a slight vibration. Then, quickly, the pressure on us begins to build. Fortunately, there is little to do. So far, everything is proceeding smoothly.

This is almost the happiest moment of my life. There are tears coming down my face. All the tensions leading up to this flight are gone. I want to enjoy every sensation.

Looking out the window I see the blue sky getting blacker and blacker as we leave Earth's atmosphere. Within twelve minutes, we are in orbit more than one hundred miles above the Earth, traveling over seventeen thousand miles an hour. At that speed, we go around the Earth in just ninety minutes. On one

Ignition of the second stage of the Saturn V rocket and separation of the first stage rocket occurred thirty-eight miles above Earth, two minutes and forty seconds after launch (*below*). The third stage shoved the Apollo spacecraft toward the moon, giving the three astronauts a spectacular view of the Hawaiian Islands (*facing page*).

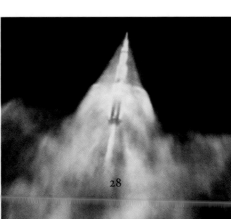

28

side of the spacecraft, we see the blue oceans of Earth. On the other, the blackness of space.

But there isn't much time to enjoy the view. We have a lot of work to do, checking out all of the systems before we head for the moon. Then there is another countdown and ignition of the third stage of the Saturn rocket. This is the TLI or Translunar Injection burn that allows us to break away from the gravitational pull of Earth and head towards the moon.

For five minutes we feel like we're riding a powerful elevator. I look out my window and see all of the Hawaiian Islands. When the rocket shuts down, we are traveling twenty-five thousand miles an hour, but there is no sensation of speed. When you ride in a car, you know you are moving because you see things going by outside the window. But in space, there are no trees or ground going by, and the Earth, moon, and stars are so far away that you don't see them move. So, though we're traveling faster than man has ever gone before, it doesn't feel like we're moving at all.

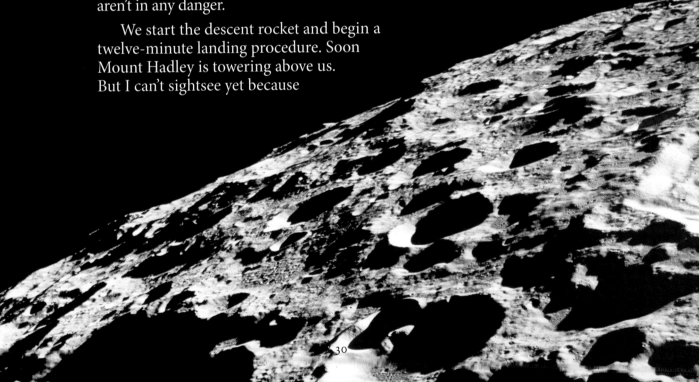

It takes us three days to fly to the moon. During this time, we have many duties, but there is also time to look back at the Earth. The Earth looks so fragile, as if it would crumble if I reached out and touched it. By the time we arrive at the moon, Earth is the size of a marble—the prettiest marble I've ever seen.

We fire an engine to slow us down so we don't fly past our destination. When we turn the rocket off, we're in an orbit around the moon. What a sight it is when we suddenly see the moon's surface for the first time. It doesn't look real. Its dark gray color makes it look like a huge lump of clay.

After orbiting the moon for a day, Dave and I put on our suits and transfer into the lunar module, which we've called *Falcon*. We find that the glass covering of the landing radar display has shattered and pieces of glass are floating around the cabin. We carefully grab the large pieces with sticky tape and hope the rest will be collected in a screen as we turn on the circulation fan.

We are eager to go down to the surface, but at first *Falcon* won't undock. It's stuck! Al has to check all of the connections, then we try again. This time it works. We move away from *Endeavour* and our orbit drops until it looks like we will crash into some of the high mountains on the moon. But that's just an illusion. The computer has everything programmed, so we aren't in any danger.

We start the descent rocket and begin a twelve-minute landing procedure. Soon Mount Hadley is towering above us. But I can't sightsee yet because

I am concentrating on our computer and other instruments, relaying information to Dave who is flying the machine.

About one hundred feet from the surface, dust begins to stir from the exhaust of our engines. There is a probe at the bottom of the landing gear, and when it touches the surface a light comes on.

"Contact!" I announce, and Dave immediately shuts down the engine. We fall the final few feet and land very hard. "Bam!" I exclaim.

For a moment, we start tilting to one side. Should we abort and take off immediately? We freeze until the *Falcon* stops moving. We have landed on the rim of a small crater. But we are safe! We hold our breath for a few more moments until mission control says we're cleared to stay.

The Apollo missions provided spectacular, never-before-seen views of Earth. The top photo on the opposite page shows the south polar ice cap and much of Africa and the Asian mainland. Mt. Hadley towered over *Falcon* as it landed. Lunar distances are deceiving. Though Hadley looks close, it is actually twenty miles away.

Our first lunar exploration lasts six-and-a-half hours. Before going back into the module to eat and rest, we dust each other off with a brush. Each of us has fallen a couple of times, so we're covered with a layer of fine black dust. When we remove our suits in the *Falcon* cabin, Dave and I immediately notice a strong smell like that of gunpowder. Apparently we didn't brush off all of the lunar dust, and when it's exposed to oxygen for the first time it gives off that strong odor.

When we awaken from our sleep, we discover a water leak. With directions from mission control, we fix the leak and dump the extra water into special containers. It's fortunate that our module landed at a slight angle on the rim of the crater. If it had tilted the other way, the water would have flowed into a mass of electrical equipment. That could have shorted connections, perhaps leaving us unable to lift off. We would have been stranded on the moon.

Our destination today is the base of Mount Hadley Delta. Our purpose is to find rocks that will better help us to analyze the lunar mountains. We park by Spur Crater and discover rocks of light green and brown. One rock in particular catches our attention. We've been asked to find a white rock, and there it is. It sits on a pedestal looking like a museum display.

Many people consider the photograph of Astronaut James Irwin (*facing page*) the most famous lunar photo ever taken. Pictured to the right is the white rock sitting on top of its natural pedestal. The instrument next to the rock is called a gnomon.

After a little extra sleep, we are ready for our third and final outing on the moon. The first assignment is to try and get a core sample using a lunar drill. This ten-foot-long rock sample will allow scientists to better understand what it is like under the lunar surface. But the drill gets stuck. It takes both of us heaving with all our strength to remove that core sample.

Though it is still early morning on the moon, we are beginning to feel the heat. We can't stay much longer. During our drive, Dave remarks, "Look at the mountains. When they're all sunlit, isn't that beautiful?"

I answer, "Dave, I'm reminded of my favorite biblical passage from the Psalms: 'I will lift up mine eyes unto the hills, from whence cometh my help.' Of course, we get quite a bit of help from Houston." I know I am also getting help from another source, the very Lord Jesus Christ who created the moon upon which we are standing.

Back at the base, Dave does "The Galileo Experiment" in honor of the famous scientist who discovered the principles of gravity. Galileo believed that, without any air, all objects, regardless of size and weight, would fall at the same speed. So Dave holds up a hammer and a feather and drops them

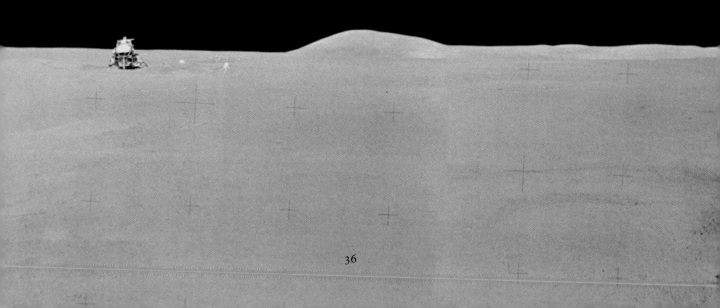

Jim Irwin left a plaque (*above*) on the moon in memory of fourteen NASA astronauts and USSR cosmonauts who had died. The tiny, manlike object represents the figure of a fallen astronaut/cosmonaut.

at the same time. Sure enough, in the airless environment, the hammer and feather float-fall at the same rate and hit the ground 1.3 seconds later.

Now it's time to start packing for the trip home. But first I have a few unplanned minutes. I run around the lunar module and do some broad jumps—in short, act like a kid. Boy, that's fun!

Then I stop and think about where I am. I'm in awe of what man has accomplished through technology. But something else is happening in me. As I look around at God's creation, I have an overwhelming sense of His presence. I feel God is calling me to Himself, and that He will give me a new mission when this one is completed.

Lift-off from the moon was recorded by the TV camera on Rover (*above left and middle*). A few minutes later, Astronauts Irwin and Scott spotted the command and service modules (*above right*). The service module contained sophisticated cameras that photographed much of the lunar night and day. Hadley Rille (*facing page, left*) was photographed from lunar orbit after *Falcon* rejoined *Endeavour*.

There is a lot of work to do before lift-off. We store the rocks and soil samples. The weight of the rocks means we must leave behind some items we don't need. We leave a big trash bag with the empty containers from our meals. Rover has to stay behind, too. I don't like the thought that our campsite is strewn with things we don't need.

We've left some souvenirs, including a coin with the fingerprints of my four children. It's strange to realize that our footprints and the other items may be here until the end of time. By the way, if you want a good used car, you know where to find one.

We're so busy that we almost miss lift-off. Fortunately, the computer doesn't forget. The ascent stage engine fires automatically, soundling like a whistling wind. One moment we are on the moon, the next we are a hundred feet above the surface. I take one last look and see the descent stage, Rover, the scientific base, and all the tracks we've made.

It takes only seven minutes before we shut down the engine and are in orbit around the moon. Now we have to find the command module. Meanwhile, we are weightless again, and all the lunar dust starts floating. I'm glad we have our helmets on so it doesn't get into our eyes.

Carefully we approach *Endeavour*. There is a dull thud as the two modules dock. Al opens his hatch and says, "Welcome home!"

Of course, we are still 250,000 miles from Earth. We transfer the valuable lunar samples into the command module, then jettison *Falcon*. It's kind of sad to know that our faithful lunar module will crash into the moon. But we can't afford to carry it back with us.

For the first time in the trip, I feel very tired. Mission control tells us all to get some much-needed sleep.

We spend two more days in lunar orbit before heading back to Earth. This allows us to take some special photographs. Many of these photographs will help NASA decide the site of future lunar landings.

When we are on the sunny side of the moon, it is uncomfortably hot, even in our underwear. On the dark side, it cools down to a comfortable temperature. About the time we are getting comfortable, we come back to the sunlit side.

One of the most critical moments of the entire trip is what is called the Trans-Earth Injection Burn. This occurs behind the moon where we are unable to communicate with Houston. The rocket must fire at exactly the right moment to release us from the moon's gravity and shove us back toward Earth. We also have to be directed at just the right angle so we don't skip off the Earth's atmosphere back into space or burn up like a shooting star. Fortunately, our equipment is very reliable, and the burn goes perfectly.

The highlight of our trip home is Al's walk in space. He has to retrieve the film used in cameras on the service module, which we jettison before entering Earth's atmosphere. When we open the hatch, it's like a vacuum cleaner sucking out everything that's loose. My toothbrush and a camera start floating out into space. Fortunately, I am able to grab them, but I do lose a comb.

I lean out of the spacecraft as Al takes his walk in space. What a sight! I'm looking out into absolute blackness. Because there is so much light from the sun, I can't see any stars and the Earth is only a thin crescent. It's a strange and wonderful experience.

For Al, this is the highlight of his trip. He describes how directly behind me is a brilliant full moon. He wants to stay out and enjoy the beautiful sight. I can't wait to get back into the security of our spacecraft.

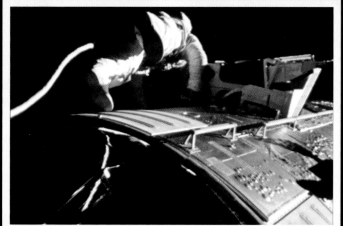

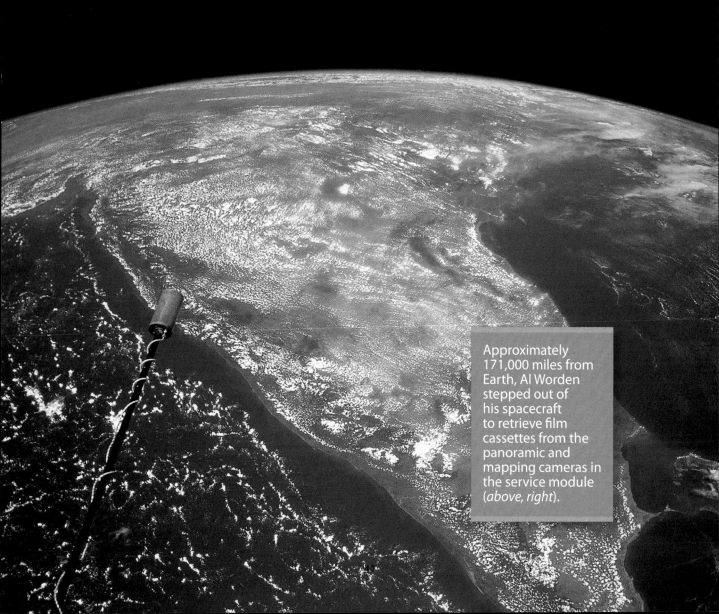

Approximately 171,000 miles from Earth, Al Worden stepped out of his spacecraft to retrieve film cassettes from the panoramic and mapping cameras in the service module (*above, right*).

The biggest shock when we return to Earth is going from weightlessness to eight Gs (eight times Earth gravity) during reentry. For about four minutes, it is impossible to lift an arm. Even breathing is difficult.

At fifty thousand feet above the ocean, a drogue parachute comes out to slow our descent. At ten thousand feet, three large chutes open. Except one of the chutes fails, so we're falling faster than expected. For a moment, I'm afraid we might have a tragic end to our trip.

We hit the water hard, and instantly I hit a switch releasing the chutes so they won't pull *Endeavour* over.

We go underwater for a moment, then pop back up like a giant cork. We're back on Earth!

Navy frogmen quickly surround the module and wave to us through the window. When they open the hatch, we pile out into a life raft. A helicopter lowers a net which lifts each of us up. A few minutes later, we're on an aircraft carrier greeting NASA officials, congressmen, generals, and admirals.

At first it is a little hard to walk because we've been in space for twelve days, experiencing weightlessness for most of the time. However, it sure feels great to be home! And we don't have to go into quarantine. For the first three Apollo missions, the crew spent three weeks in isolation to make sure they were not carrying any unknown germs back to Earth. But scientists have decided that it is safe to touch us.

Our work isn't finished yet. We have several weeks of debriefing, where we tell scientists and NASA officials everything we learned on our trip. We also need time to recover physically and be united with our families. Then we visit our President and take a trip around the world, telling people about what we saw on the moon.

Apollo 15's return to Earth had a little extra excitement when one of the parachutes failed to open. However, the astronauts arrived home safely to a warm reunion with family and friends. Meanwhile, analysis began on the 170 pounds of lunar rock and soil samples from the mission. Each sample was weighed, measured, and classified before going to scientists around the world for study.

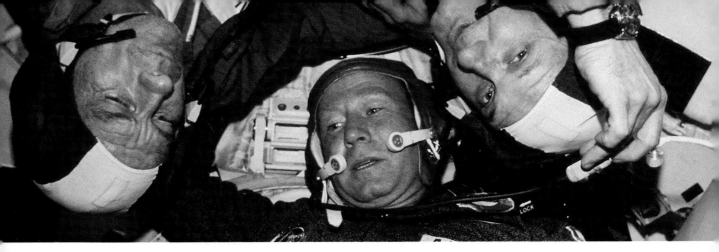

Ever since the historic mission of Apollo 15, I've been telling people about my trip. That includes my spiritual experience, for what happened to me on the moon changed my life forever. Before the trip, I was so absorbed with preparations that I never thought how high the spiritual flight could be. Now I believe God wanted me to go to the moon so I could come back and do something more important with my life than fly airplanes or a spacecraft. That's why I now travel anywhere in the world that people will have me—to tell them about my trip and also about my relationship with God.

Many men and women have flown into space since my flight. There were two more trips to the moon. There was the Sky Lab project where astronauts worked for many months in space. There was a joint flight where an Apollo capsule linked up with a Soyez spacecraft from the Soviet Union. The Soviets have set up a space station where cosmonauts can work for a year at a time. And of course, there are the American and Soviet space shuttles that put satellites in orbit and conduct important experiments. Our knowledge grows with every trip we take.

What is the future of space travel? One real possibility is a trip to Mars. Who knows, perhaps you will be one of the crew members. Or perhaps you will journey to farther reaches of our solar system, to Jupiter or beyond.

A few years ago, such thoughts were impossible dreams. But they aren't anymore. In fact, they're far more possible than my crazy dream of going to the moon when I was a boy. So don't be afraid to dream big dreams. Yes, shoot for the stars!

But I think it's even more important to recognize the Creator of this great planet and the universe in which it exists. After all, He is the one who created the laws of science that make space travel possible. With God in control of our lives, not only can we explore other planets, we have hope for this planet. With His help, you and I can have a part in making Earth a better place for all of us.

A lot has happened in space since the flights to the moon. One of the last Apollo flights was a joint venture with the Soviet Union (*facing page*). In the 1980s, the Space Shuttle became the primary space vehicle while the Soviet Union and United States plotted more distant destinations. Perhaps the twenty-first century will see manned flights to Mars (*left, upper middle*), Jupiter (*lower middle*), or even Saturn (*bottom*).

Seventeen years after the flight of Apollo 15, James Irwin made a special presentation to General Secretary Mikhail Gorbachev of the Soviet Union. Jim took the Soviet flag with him as a small token of the tremendous achievements of the Soviet space program.

Photo Credits: All photos provided courtesy of the National Aeronautics and Space Administration unless otherwise noted. **Page 4:** (*left*) TASS from Sovofoto; (*right*) Mercury 4. **Page 5:** (*top and middle*) John Glenn, Mercury 6; (*bottom left*) Alan Shepard, Mercury 3; (*bottom right*) Gemini 4. **Pages 6,7:** YF-12A courtesy of Department of Defense Still Media Records. **Page 6:** Portrait of Irwin, July 1971. **Page 7:** Astronauts Class of 1966. **Page 8,9:** Centrifuge photos from Manned Spacecraft Center, Houston, Texas. Jungle training class, June 1967, and Geology training, July 1967. **Page 10:** Zero gravity training, February 1967; Apollo 15 Water Egress training. **Page 11:** Gemini 12 underwater training. **Page 12:** (*top*) Apollo 1 fire; (*bottom*) LTA-8 testing. **Page 13:** (*top*) Jim Irwin, LTA-8; (*middle*) James Irwin, foreground, and Grumman Aircraft Engineering pilot, LTA-8; (*bottom*) Test subject Robert Piljay prior to start of LTA-8 tests. **Page 14:** (*left*) Apollo 15 being moved to launch pad; (*top and bottom, right*) Apollo 10 Assembly. **Page 15:** (*top*) Apollo Critical Design Review activity, February 1966; (*bottom*) Apollo Command Module controls, April 1966. **Page 16:** Apollo Training Facility, Manned Spacecraft Center, Houston, Texas. **Page 17:** Apollo 13. **Page 18:** (*top and left*) Apollo 15; (*right*) Desert survival training, August 1967. **Page 19:** (*left*) Equipment test, February 1970; (*middle*) Lunar simulation, April 1965; (*right*) Apollo 15; (*top*) Apollo 15 crew, March 1971. **Page 20:** Rover license provided courtesy of Ferenc Pavlics and General Motors; Rover practice, Apollo 15. **Page 21:** (*top*) Command Module interior, May 1967, courtesy of North American Aviation, Inc.; (*middle*) Apollo 9 lunar module simulator training; (*bottom*) Apollo 15 EVA simulation. **Page 22:** Apollo landing sites. **Page 23:** Apollo 15. **Pages 24,25:** Apollo 15. **Pages 26,27:** Apollo 15. **Page 28:** (*bottom, left and right*) Apollo 11. **Pages 28,29:** Apollo 15. **Page 29:** Space Shuttle, October 1988. **Page 30:** (*top*) Apollo 17; (*bottom*) Apollo 11. **Page 31:** Apollo 15. **Pages 32,33:** Apollo 15. **Pages 34,35:** Apollo 15. **Pages 36,37:** Apollo 15. **Page 38:** (*top*) Apollo 17; (*background*) Apollo 15. **Page 39:** Apollo 15. **Pages 40,41:** Apollo 15. **Page 42:** Apollo 15 lunar samples. **Page 43:** Apollo 15. **Page 44:** Apollo-Soyuz, July 1975. **Page 45:** (*top, left*) Space Shuttle *Challenger*, April 1984; (*second, left*) Viking Lander 2; (*third, left*) Voyager 1; (*bottom, left*) Voyager 2; (*background*) Space Shuttle *Challenger*, August 1983. **Page 46:** Associated Press Photo.

A special thank you to Lisa Vasquez-Morrison, still photo researcher at NASA Lyndon B. Johnson Space Center.

The discovery of God's creation is one of the greatest gifts given to man by his Creator. To learn more about what the Bible has to say about the moon and all of creation, please consider some of the following resources:

Jonathan Park Creation Radio Drama

Families will delight to this internationally broadcast radio drama, about a family of Christians and scientists who explore creation for the glory of God. Fast-paced, exciting, and chock-full of important spiritual and scientific lessons for the family, *Jonathan Park* is sure to delight listeners of all ages. For a list of stations near you, or to download home school lesson plans based on subjects covered in the radio drama, visit:

www.jonathanpark.com

The Vision Forum, Inc.

For a wide range of creation products including biblical and scientific literature about the moon and all of creation, visit the Web store of The Vision Forum, Inc., a company dedicated to the preservation and strengthening of the Christian family in the twenty-first century.

www.visionforum.com
1-800-440-0022
4719 Blanco Rd.
San Antonio, TX 78212

Vision Forum Ministries

Vision Forum Ministries is dedicated to rebuilding the culture of the Christian family. This includes training men and women to build their worldview on God's Word. For a list of resources, free downloadable articles, and conferences (including "Back to Genesis" creation conferences), visit their Web site at:

www.visionforum.org

Answers in Genesis

For scientific and biblical answers to thousands of questions about creation, please visit Answers in Genesis, an organization dedicated to equipping Christians to defend the faith in this secular/scientific age. Answers in Genesis is building a major Creation Museum in the Greater Cincinnati area to reach out to Christians and non-Christians alike. More information on this ministry and Creation Museum can be found at:

www.answersingenesis.org
(800) 350-3232
P.O. Box 510
Hebron, KY 41048

The Institute for Creation Research

For more than thirty-five years, the Institute for Creation Research has been the trailblazer in leading scientific research and discovery. Their international team of scientists have produced thousands of papers, books and radio shows, including numerous examples of groundbreaking research, on the all important topic of science and the Bible. Founded by Dr. Henry Morris, and now under the leadership of his son Dr. John Morris, ICR continues to set a standard of excellence for creation science.

www.icr.org
(619) 448-0900
10946 Woodside Ave. N.
Santee, CA 92071

ASTRONAUT COL. JIM IRWIN'S HIGH FLIGHT FOUNDATION

Oh! I have slipped the surly bonds of Earth
And danced the skies on laughter-silvered wings;
Sunward I've climbed, and joined the tumbling mirth
Of sun-split clouds—and done a hundred things
You have not dreamed of—wheeled and soared and swung
High in the sunlit silence. Hov'ring there
I've chased the shouting wind along, and flung
My eager craft through footless halls of air.
Up, up the long delirious, burning blue,
I've topped the windswept heights with easy grace
Where never lark, or even eagle flew—
And, while with silent lifting mind I've trod
The high untrespassed sanctity of space,
Put out my hand and touched the face of God.

PILOT JOHN GILLESPIE MAGEE, JR.
No. 412 Squadron, RCAF
Killed December 11, 1941

Inspired by the moving words of the poem "High Flight" by John Gillespie Magee, Jr., Apollo 15 Astronaut James B. Irwin adopted the title for the name of a unique foundation he started, dedicated to giving hope and inspiration to the next generation of adventurers. In the years following his retirement from NASA in 1972, Col. Irwin launched the High Flight Foundation.

Through High Flight Foundation, Col. Irwin traveled the world sharing with audiences the exciting details of his adventure to the mountains of the moon. Col. Irwin loved to travel. For nearly twenty years to almost every country in the world, he would take his shiny silver Haliburton suitcases, his big bag of oats, his film (from the Apollo 15 flight), and friends and family members to join him as he recounted the glory, honor, and privilege of being one of only twelve people in all of human history to walk on the moon.

Though he died in 1991, High Flight Foundation is still active today, honoring the memory and achievements of Col. James Irwin and Apollo 15 by sharing his experience with children across the nation and beyond via Project Uplift. High Flight is also privileged to present to the leaders and representatives of different countries, the very flags of their nations that were taken to the moon on Apollo 15. Through High Flight Foundation, the children, family, and friends of Col. Irwin continue to advance his legacy of encouragement to young and old, with the message that we must never give up on noble and godly dreams.

To contact High Flight Foundation, write to:

High Flight Foundation
P.O. Box 62532
Colorado Springs, CO 80962
(719) 641-0861